FUEL

ROSIE STOCKTON

FUEL
ROSIE STOCKTON

NIGHTBOAT BOOKS
NEW YORK

Copyright © 2025 by Rosie Stockton

All rights reserved
Printed in the United States

ISBN: 978-1-64362-274-3

Design and typesetting by Rissa Hochberger
Typeset in Bembo

Cataloging-in-publication data is available
from the Library of Congress

Nightboat Books
New York
www.nightboat.org

These are my shoes, but are these my lack of
Shoes?
That is, is my shoelessness mine?

—Bernadette Mayer, "Soule Sermon"

WHETHER YOU LOVE WHAT YOU LOVE

OR LIVE IN DIVIDED CEASELESS
REVOLT AGAINST IT

WHAT YOU LOVE IS YOUR FATE

—Frank Bidart, "Guilty of Dust"

CONTENTS

LOOSE ENDS

look, the earth has undermined

a World into a new state of water

one no single pair of eyes

could lay their hands on

into a charred air quality

where risk analysis vacations

now, a pulse in the ground leads me to you

when we are summoned

by the green valley

lonely, turbulent with Lexapro

& untresspassable

you stop to classify the wild roses

so we may emulate their forms

of jealousy, so we may lay down

at their feet

when there is nothing I cannot remember, I carve myself back into myself

I am the boy who can rhyme

with any body's gestures

I tie you to the rain

my only technology

the soil in heaven—

is it very strong?

can it sing in paradox?

so we may finally be bad to one another, outside this planetary death drive fragile beauty

become more remote

make decrepit of category

make ruin of taxonomy

your breath is a leash

that coils around my expanding radius

this is my impossible apocalypse

my fault line friction

the advice I heard from the prairie

and its split architecture

melodic to dine on the bricks in this estate

clock gender's badge number

burn off policed value

truthfully, I can't prove I am not a robot, but I can prove my disobedience

I open my wallet to debt's imagination

what binds my hands to yours

I give away what I have none of

in order to merge with my grief's ghosts

I hide my social danger card

whose digits spill off the paper

I hunt my generational secrets

I eat my meals when the hickory

commands me to spread its seeds

I pollinate myself, become public funds

I collapse, like wind does

ever shifting edicts, this is how

our kink must keep up

with the pace of inexplicable fear

of overripe shame

I'll always turn toward the darkened clouds, there is no way to explain luxury

Dear End,

My fall
for you is prelapsarian.

Every time I leave our dream, I am under attack.
It isn't my death they want, it is just to be inside.

It is only under a new moon I learn to take you seriously.
I leave my bed unmade, I show up late for work.

We could be many things—I could give it up,
I could tell you exactly what to do.

Shut up and shut down, baby birding communion,
transubstantiate your little joke.

Let the tips of our boots touch,
stack our books on top of one another.

I memorize your schedule. Your metaphysics rule
my circadian rhythms, my bowel movements.

I have remained committed to our private bacchanal,
left the cobwebs intact, so the breeze has something to touch,

chaotic in absent moonlight.
It softens me, it blurs my drive.

You said keep going and I kept going
long after you looked away,

CARMEN ET ERROR

[ ]

like cupid I can only shoot
one arrow at a time
but I'm practicing comrade,
I'm full of drafts. entering our
canopy, blemished and pruned,
unearthed light stumbles
through layers of orange
season's particulate, having
never wanted to invade
anyone's oblivion, but there
was no other place.

we could live here, I think, and we do.
in this mansion-like fallowed
field where I see you
unask why May gloom
makes the golden air feel
so fertile and extracted.

all premeditation, all the ways
I know harm are legal,
all this care knows no redress
from surplussed nematodes that jack
down the price of how we live
in this strict orchard whimsy.

I needed you
to fortify this need
with water rights, secure
applauding clouds of dust,
invent the clock and clock

out, enter muffled horizons.
I needed you exiled
outside perfection, thickly
peeled, an Ovidian error I keep
close to my mirror, dwelling with
me obscenely, eyes trained on
that slippery double, the
reservoir's chemical fish
enact their own epic,
redact the rehearsal
& bow out.

[ ]

you petition my potable void
I come this way because my mother—
was she never thirsty? I feel out my splayed
source, my private shade of bioblush

I'm just tenor carrying tenor, broken
down truck revamped my dream
glowing with my losses
how forever happened yesterday
how they tried to contain my ground water

the poems you have in your life
make me feel like I am not a god
when I authorize you to authorize me
I get this whole new end of the world

        I let what I hurt carry me
        I risk unaccountable heat
        I get as breakable as possible

only then could unison whisper
to me. come with us—ethicked
beauty, unarmed eyes

we're perfecting hysteria
so beauty can finally desire us

[ ]

the fact is
I belong to order
but disorder belongs to us

& I long for it, disposable
delusion, what I'm wanting
to untame, how I'm kept
alive in your unrest

amplifying my term, twirling
here and there, making myself made
of money. easy selling
dirt, all of it

comes from the cave in me
thick mud walls and methods
of replenishing water I don't understand

it could almost hurt
I think, if I could touch the light

when I jump in deep enough
I become part of the ensemble, it tempts me,
I drag my feet along the receding bottom

in the river you touched my hip and I turned
effortlessly, the water coldest at midnight,
gathered around mud's disappearing swallow

I would have many expectations of you, disorderly
stepping back, wanting you
not to refuse my famous limits, my certain knots

when my gaze falls away
it is because I'm unprepared to break
you, despite my intent. I coax the tick
into a jar, thighs fresh and unslept

      in the mornings I trash my spam
      but never unsubscribe

[ ]

parked in the velocity of possible

a blockaded we
gets me going, splash
scaled up

like gravity, a humid force
crawling beyond
consequence

of redistro'd masses
curving out a new space
time, not owning my own
yell, I whisper many smashed
mantras opening to love
inefficien-
cy

downtown tonight
I latch onto our
geodesic deviation, rounding
spring + first for the second time

there I trashed my poem, made up
my own constraints
to disobey

right in the here & now
I sign up for this touchability
training, becoming
all at once un-

touchable & so explodable
no archy could account for

a brutality in the breeze's
order, facing a redacted lurch
while a ballistic comms
thread names me
cryptolegible to myself
a transcendental
anybody,

adminning the pooling
salt, so when we turn
our heads, we turn

them together, knowing
that's not self
policing, that's auto-
chory, a sonic splinter,

a temperate and pappus coming
apart

[ ]

gassed up, coalesced

my clingy neurons
feelingly over
burdened, scan the
official errata & let me know
how come in the big scheme
of things, I came
to watch the perennial
artichoke plant snap fast &
purple under its own weight

there, against all my upended will
I became an echo waiting
to be let into the aftermath
of attachment

like a limp margin
enclosure, their tactics fry
my commonsense,
heighten my submerged decay

fist gusty, I dip
all ways to choke out
my inner acclaim, fill
my mood with daily filth

get beggy and meditative
unhanded pleasure trust

let loose
all discordant drives
& as my longing list approaches
this impending maturation

I'm like tear it up reality
loot my lay of the land

gather my ways of loving
what lets go of me
too soon

[ ]

escalate me, idyllic chores
encrypt this little bruised soul of mine

sublimate the kitchen floor
till it's squeaky clean

is there room for our future harms
in this uncommon demos?

sent myself an invite
wrote myself to rsvp

[ ]

we got vacuum sealed
in the eye of the windowpane

the backside
of alone

love is famous so let's drink
from a different fountain

the breath's audience
the off staged thing

Dear End,

Like I promised, I haven't lied
nor told a single truth in weeks.

You said truth can no longer be the operative framework
between us, if we are to witness each other rightly.

My only touchable fact is a frozen
dream seamed out to consummate

my waxing moon, that took the pomegranate
out of my body for one vertiginous minute.

But only you know that,
how my fingers roll each jewel from its rind.

I took your name to the bath, I took your name on a walk,
I smashed your name in the toilet.

I offered it to city infrastructure.
An expression of my devotion.

Ritual induces rupture. I cultivate weeds,
I tend our security. I am waiting, weighing

your technique in my mouth, attention
hovering over the slabbed concrete.

The previous tenant's curtains
block your light from my eye.

In wanting you, all becomes you.
Midnight wraps around us,

when we can finally be together—
our horizon exists only in destruction of time,

EMERGENCY

this poem to be plundered   to tremble down a belted slide   to make a hole
     in the World   thrown to the wind   shown to you   that I know   Nothing

of hands & broken seals   Nothing divining quality   controlling bacterial rhymes
     a projectile chant touches itself   that joy machine   cursing out the cure here

where we've got scanned facts   and nowhere to put them   but the extinguished
     sunlight   our love & logistics   play truth or dare   our rituals write me

famously alive   these neural pathways I walk along   memorizing wild flower
     after wild flower   while you   make flammable bouquets   of all the heat

     I've never felt   that permeate the ground water   that write me shattered

a palliative shame is all in you honey   that long slow stream   combed and crystalized
     to feel our pressurized limit   this broken up thing   *where we became what we beheld*

godly   how love rendered me   useless, uses me wrong   but this below all:
     you don't owe me anything   but me   and when you possess the emergency

                    make it kinetic   then detonate that prayer

two things   that can't be alone together   sun & the tree's shadow
      a death concept   multiplied the light   that keeps me up   at night

conservationist on vacation   where my cavity mind was worth   all that sweetness
      & in it you look phony good   like with one look   you could   separate

the carbon dioxide from the stratosphere   today even the billboards are on rent strike
      & no one knows   what to buy   or what could induce   our uncontainable future

                  no debt   no bedtime   no love   that burns off its limit

it's difficult to break the bonds   you don't know you have   let's get brilliant
      and choke em out   bad grades in the arid zone   of how it happens

how it's happening   *all* the *time*   this stream of info and sunlight   pouring in—
      but me?   I've got nothing to invade   cuz I'm all outside myself

                  & if you can capture it   it isn't *it*   anymore

that demo solved something for me   clicked me into place   & now I'm taking
      selfies again   lipping through my sins and zoom options   ready to troll it

fellow faggots   our Love   starts the riot of my eye's collagen   totally atonal

if my picture makes it bearable   I crumple fruity   prepared to bear more
     beyond max capacity   we are living in drag time   never tomorrow   I steep

privately   repetition compulsion   how all money is oil money   and surplus
     fields capture surplus gender   with surplus justice absorbing   fallowed life

pumped from the cut up groundwater   spliced   rationed   & sold
     layers of land incised deep   cored out lack blinds   whitelife echoing

          pleasantly packaged   atrocity

that's the   uncorporeal slurp up I hear   the future market   calculates an all too
     related execution   of wealth's protection   O gee I joe haunted that one

little mole   framed the out of frame   annotated all things   left me unthinking
     hard   in strobe light   of the unmourned   spoil spill   cleaned up category

          of extraction   &   defense spending

with you   I bear more   commit an unmeasuring   time's weight   only measured
     by the club's cut   and the thing that's in the way   do we both want to see it?

          earth's redaction   each sip is its own tome

hinge   open   an   ocean   cast out of private   mystical experience
    in my parent's   basement I became a telepath   inheriting doom

the duration of child's play   let me now   know   why could I suddenly appear
    in a pile of toxic dirt   why could I suddenly   shift a half-life

                        made of gridlocked spores   unexplodable

& let light be   genuinely unnamable!   apostle shit   only if I was un buried
    un truth procedure   could I fly tears   & cry away   could I be all of time

                    my categories   archived promenade

        in this gauntlet, I fear how to live. living gauntlet, the unseen hand
        rumbles without fear. I drink in to have lived, unhanded water
        dissolves fear. I can't fall as far as fear lives, some gauntlet protects
        no hands. living proof of a sonnet's fear. is she born with it? living?
        I fear where I am going you don't need fear. where I am from, there is
        only subtle living. a lifeworld's bacterial factory, only ever edging fear.
        to   live   with   it   all   here,   the   fear   leasing   me.

karmic promise: the gas fireplace can't crackle   but it can obscure my shadows
    nonetheless   I'm exposed sense   limit after limitafterlimit strip

this happy dream an   excuse to see you   I'm stunned listening   metal conducts
    the sunset and clouds come to dry me off   the body that stole   away my body

that presence   cutting edge   mothering glassware   cracked and exempt
    gilded, it breaks me   all glass and simultaneity   all cloud   could be so similar

is that how you want to ask me?   take a bite of it   it is steam   and an ask   to fall forever

30

re fuse   the science   light up   how the text itself conceals pre cinct
    encircled body   sharp melancholy receiving   shamefaced splash   to salvage

a blossoming No   all gut   all care and full   all dancing   engaged fantasy
    to pass thru hands   & wouldn't we unhave?   we would in the cracks. would

crack   and lean outside   the cracking to splinter separation   to flood whitetime
    & pre/serve difference outside of self   where passive gravity becomes agency

                I duck the map's irreparable weight. unauthorized, unauthorable
                slowed down so much a *we* gets swallowed in coalition's embers, not
                to walk the coals, but to disperse spilled heat footing the partial dream
                of we becoming ups the anti- to provoke an ante- care, overlapping
                radial glow tricking the gridlocked archive, the trouble bubbles over
                lies in subjunctive de subjective rhythms a brutal would to rewire de-
                sire's rampages and blush beyond a spiny chill, how yesterday is all time

gathering speed   in arms   undueled velocity to centrifuge the   *arch I have*
    that has written aloneness   interrupted to spread   it's the unlinkedchainlink

bolt cutter loving   in a silence or sounding surround unpossesses the   World
    to find world   to walk slow   to gather the battered sea reckless & soft

where it hurts a shadow's warring self- sources   a large ache   this acre of cosmic
space   release a bound gazing   leashed down   lease deranged   to feed the garden

whose closed eyes see best   after image glow   all sound floods history's property
    excess redressed up   spike an idle view & treasure the refusing every labor cries

presence! in this lifetime   forging beauty & hunger
    insurgent grief   collaborates with a water's   unleasable joy

31

unshorn and should have charged more   tonight my clementine peels   itself for me
    & my truck takes too long to start   parked on 8 mile   behind neon class war

like vodka   I know how to let it drive me home   rattled my motorjaw on 1k nights
    mowing baby truths   spruced w salt water gin   but Absinthe taught me to always

fake the shot   I've made good use   of my splashy death drive   docked
    and warped jersey   jean   and pressed cotton   of my mystic tricks   who fashion

repetition more melodic   a villanelle   to swerve hunger   a good fucking duck
    O gaseous bulb   so unlit   your waist hummock deep   waded into a pitcher plant

        that promising trap   enzymes up in arms

    I talk to you. sleep crawls thick, reliable. little puddles ache, there are
    bugs trying to live too. they can. we struck a deal. we are all eyes to
    the sky, perforated with cirrus clouds. it splits us gently, I take baths
    just so water wears down what's jagged. as close as I can get to a rip
    tide. purging your names I make one hundred vows just to break them
    all. gave up giving things up. as if prohibition could do anything but gas
    pedal it. I talk to you. I keep talking to you. it's not love that we give up.
    it's being bound to days.

the cashier's velvet laws occult and friendly   fold my nerves, because how else to oil
    time? when you clean up good, we rinse each other   ball bearings on strike

enlisting aloof Corps   & doubling down on fatty vengeance Rolex value hacking
    but when you doth protest this much, our contract uninvents us   plumbed a tense

sentence that could never drench enough to fill   the nightshift's gullet   sprawling
    janky signifiers upcharged   & bounced extras looming—   no, blooming— large

        pour one out for the nervous system   for it's older   than the soul

Dear End,

I keep wishing my own plurality,
but get hailed back into this self.

My dreams make their own ending for love.
I could always keep going without you.

I told you, you can feel it if you want to—
everything that's ever happened—

Only then can we be governed rightly—
where metaphor becomes transubstantiation.

You're unresisting, an image of our day.
All things press and clap. Wrapping belt, a clunky suitcase.

Where are you now?
I like not to know, but only to ask.

You play hard to get
only because in our love, there is no having.

Tiny prose, precise scam.
A minor be mine…

Unveiled devastation, if there was anything
to reveal I'd be made of revelations.

I write you in the here and now,
the then and there. It's fire season again,

growing more sayable each year,
it incites me into this present.

I look for you
until I can't be more sunk.

Suddenly, and always, there will be
three of everything,

DISPERSAL

[ ]

value packs everywhere
declutter this immovable lease

I love to degrade my warring self
outclassed & dragged nasty into view
renegade humiliation
the portrait of a betrayal

I waltz borrowed after borrowed form
slam recyclables in the trash
crash efficiency off the balcony
a true Leveller, luddite core

today I slow down
time and plant gold to dig, cancel future,
check my views, look for you

it's chore day & I boil your packer
melting your biggest lack
unstuffed and sorry, the scams
you inspire in me, tidy and daddy

I wake you asking do you think we really
exist today? humming undust me

I kiss your yawn
agape or asleep, I got free
fall

we get along so great
but you throw away what I'd keep forever

deep dive to a sudden
crevice, how you scrump the edges
low hanging possession
so intricately ours
unlike all this private fucking
property, where maggots make soil,
rats scamper on the newly built fence
hoarding bursting fruit

that I don't pick, I simply suck
what's growing on the branch

[ ]

you swim to the other side
of our lake made of only dust
and cloud residue

the sun touches your surface & I
relax into a derealized state
where you can't remember
what you forgot

from here there's a good view
of how this brown water
is unsurprisingly here

it's that simple
there is no way to agree

     I finger a bur
     I want to be nothing
     but of things

     & if I am more me
     next to you
     it's because relation
     made me this way

like light, you hit me
when I ask you to

I let flood emboss me
I dress up straw men
just to find new ways

to love all I extravagantly
destroy

braced for fire season
all that makes us
possible, before our candle
swallows the wick
and that summer darkness drenches us
   here, I feel the story so many ways
   I have to lay down

[ ]

like a line that doesn't Regulate
I edge commonly

our verge retrieved the most daily feeling
your Orbit dragged me
       picnicked in my
       altitude

defining joints, I explore abrupt logic
to faster's limit   a supporting support

where no law   begins to say
       my *wish I was*

consider a layer's flux Expression—

that's my wavelength
flaunting my freedom threshold

tide line thinner based enough to lift math
to eliminate this halo fade

too thin to support
even every boundary

a glow
that ignores surface light

sitting here with you, I thought
why not accept the hurdle

float a lifted constitution

        place myself kindly

        in your slow gravity

[ ]

searing toxic, flooded sky
total absent undulation
gathers the poured lot and
state's genocidal parking fee
where love's off gasses blow
out a tire with my digital
memory and filthy fucking
hands

that's the road
all over me
that's the wallet
flying off the roof that's
my everything, lost twice
the same way but
touch it, the pooling
how I spread
out my Everything
between you the dog and
the chemical foam hunting
fish beckoned to glance
a reddish horizon takes
my breath up and atom

we are the only people
today shrugging stunning
how the stolen Snake River
confronts stone
volcanic battery life
surges hungry snacks
litter my lining

strained for you
this is loving. I walk so
fast wanting water
eddies to ghost, wanting
to point myself out
to you, there, there
and there

[   ]

a colossal water turned
me out, turned me
ordinary, a violet
authority rented my
ruler, an unverified
directrix to play dead
alongside, as I track
your soft swerve against
my will

our conduit's tantrum
blocks me anonymous
flocking my ostrich trick
I bury this triangle
deep in a rioting rhyme:
your thistle, our cement dust,
and some filthy comet I feel

again today I'm waiting
for your call, it's my giant
secret that turns snow
erotic, daring to thaw me,
a deadlined employee
or any other gut word

that disavows my private
sphere. as usual I hold
your domino lightly, scaled
up plop to make habit
of your borrowed pace

a coming volta haunts
my worn-out brake pads:
O cloud, I've never even
shouted your name

if you had other limbs I'd
write them here. could you eat
even, with unarmed
inner life? but you really live
like this, just cavity
host, your grammar
spilling everywhere

[ ]

in company my prayers fracture
beautifully, it's alone I fear
what I am capable of, having
been released from the wave
where I love to leave
my breathing

on shore you confiscate
my orbital sander,
preserve all detail, keep
these penned shims kept
guessing, my repetition
sickness on stage

it's always in media res I snag
a trace, I find you finally
between the grains of sky,
to covet and to spare.

touching your sigh, it's light–
ning in relief, no job
too small, all favors for
you, my pleasures, crisscrossing
our separateness, our nightly forms

all this I frame:
my most three-leafed clover

and if I want you haptic
it's in many dimensions

of broached, ceaseless,
hoarded, happening
bumping staccato, pothole spasm,
parataxis, a sugar structure, combed
conjunct, beside you I could go
on and on

[ ]

needless to say
swimming upstream makes me
so right here

a sky drip frequents
each daybreak, drills
totalized futures

to hold your breeze open,
marked palm, soft pallet
in the passenger seat

to bite hard the hand
that feeds my grind.

your off-gas bounces
my glance. the epic's underside,
to demand too late
the outtakes of a workday

if there is something to be done,
could there be a beginning
buried later, if you make contact
with the world, all skin,
epi dexterous, ruthless
-logue

even so, you tie me
in a bow, gift me to all else

whetstone on
ragged absence
such useful return

to animate my want of how
we come to pass

[   ]

now they are trading
water futures, I speculate
the cost of my piss
and wait for the price
of gauged luxury air
markets to freshen the
space between my breath
and your breeze, where
there is all this subprime
business. O to be part
of no such thing feeling,
a partial eviction,
prefix menu of how loss
is in me, a tier 2 user,
playing boxcar to be
a grad of droughted alone

I save your plants my recycled bath
water, souped up dirt, dipping
in my trade, me in your
gym day, blowing our grip
on any averaged catalyst

[   ]

when I stroke the sky
it's to shuck dad's genre

cast a shadow net
to bless the digested

mollusk, colony bent
toward every singular

pleasure. velvet dirt a
then carcassed tech–

nique of spinal cord
to rot and bloom

nothing but roots.
disordered scent:

the most accurate
preservation of chaos.

vulture spreading
dive in the state shallows

to bleed out cloud
a now'd tomorrow is all over me

clocking
the thinness of sails
the thickness of wind

[ ]

you are on the couch
with someone else's hell

on your tongue. I'm longing
for an argument to crack up

our geodic unit and rock me
into a glistening separateness

that lets us
in a little more

the problem with distance
is that it just works too good

    & when I understand it, I don't
    believe in it anymore

Dear End,

When I look at you it's rarely with proper grammar.
I dreamed you picked up the entire pew and turned

toward me. You betrayed your pulpit.
My gaze stationed direct,

a holy ghost in the slow deluge of my habit.
Then, you sat silently, to call me out.

You are always looking for some far-off cinderblock to seduce,
to be loyal to by never speaking its name.

I enflesh our difference,
I feel the busy movements of our void.

I don't want you superimposed; I want
to bridge this filthy yearning.

I feel I have earned this,
your distance, your intimacy.

I undo myself, therefore I am.
I create a theory of noticing you.

I can feel when you think of me,
when our eye lands on the same star.

Some days I get so lonely,
I clean the fridge of our associations.

I destroy our state. I start anew on our braids.
I say my evening prayer: May we slip away unnoticed.

The silences in the archive
are not the silences in heaven,

CONTACT POTENTIAL

[　]

you're a bound cloud
mist locked down   skipped
across the lake, I can tell

I woosh your eye's pallet
missing calls   flatten
hunger   a slow drawl
boy with backseat taste
buds exploited by fire

just so you keep coming
utterly west

boxy glam and fresh anguish
buffing the sun   if I slam

your door   it's only to look
away   to prepare my gutter

batten down my hatches
for a solar trip   where for
me you   reside in Chiron's
wound   decadent dare

shaved   till barely dusk, I refuse
your food   replenish you
perfectly dead   plug up
your promise dream

till the   silt of our river bed

[ ]

secret, seek me,
voyager for you

I will never forget
my perfected will
blown out gaze that cuts

corners, rotund & proud
of my diagram
that contains our
flows, a vertical
pleasure against all
principal

it's how I teeter
so you stay put for me

& disobey
on cue

my little grid
ground down
I'll shove you law like
walking while essence
shadow banned golden
rod, the Ovidian void
of my syllabi

I've been taught
for so long I have no choice
but to relax all strings

how quietly
I play you

imperturbable lake, plowed
glassy, bound northern, plucked
jam, wilting inside
my summer, unbundled
all over my dock

[   ]

your guided veils always
losing vaster losing further

like water I gather
your loose ends up in my
barely braided arms
to usher this crown acting up

I get made alive during this transit
four times your garden
variable divine and owned
training to fluster my next to last

your arrivals untie today
to brace me, noticing
nixed fiction, wishing dirt
fixed disaster, where you

maybe see the outside in
my body, remove me
from time, cull spores, be
flower, be, breath, pay me

attention, revenge gifts get
impossibly locked
down, pilling fragrance

you spew high speed read
skimming on the kitchen
floor, doing my dusty dishes

incompatibly inflected jewel
resting on my pulse

it's not just your gaze that lasts
my all day, you soft new terror
surfaced ploy, waking chain
tangled, ghosting for each
other, sunned and sunning

      here I go showing you
      my symptom to lose you
      faster, but I can't catch it
      any other way

[   ]

O host itch,
all guest talk

tend my ambient scope
spare me operative
never fully included
but I like my spell
doxing conduit, tell-all
at attention, proof
of ill-will

O bother
tote stain
O luna
bar crash hard

waxing fuel plummet
when the chill falls
your tantrum fluffs
the pillows, I gift you a
kill drive, your clock's
lady in waiting game,
unload a should or shouldn't
you break here

O dogged
the glittering

week that rends time
open, to fill with baggy
dirt, to plant a start

in the all day long.
skilled in all ways
contending

     O you're
     a townload

sacking my secret,
man of twists
and returns

[ ]

yes
gerund, curl up
in my direct address

you need an allergy
pill, and yes, I do too.

you describe my private
verbs, clatter locked in
your joints, sniff and gash,
shop and scatter
my regiment.

as our bind
steeps in a weekly
debt fall before a last
ditch Venmo request,
you look at me
like I'm good for it.

yes
garden you are here
to be a perfect poem.

yes scissors in your hair
cutting up time like you do

booked by the job search
unslept ribbons marching
mania to a classical rave.

yes you never forget
the bag, pope shit, my holy
committee.

yes
pit in my pit
I'm late just like you
like it

[ ]

villainous spaghetti, you couldn't be
farther from my station

a stain on my void
glance the drycleaner's offer

reluctantly I blot
w tidepooling tidepen

what's the difference between
work-from-home and staycation?

I only work for pleasure,
I taste each sip's praise

as career careens
we evict the mansions

detoxing prefabbed design
the pouring rain governs our station

I duck any oncoming praise
gather my drives to jam the margin

any bender to bring you closer
to my design

lyric and bursting, this body's
my offer, it reeks of praise

infecting flame, alive in a margin
I take up your station, decay like a mansion

[ ]

bratty planets rule my grammar

my mother's chance
demanded maudlin sprees

it was in a complete sentence
the first time I sulked

emasculating Mars barely flanks
my timeline

destroying punishment,
object attached

rules gang up on my joviality

ever since I was born under land
decisively Saturn spoke

to the fullest reflection of our drastic
roll over, and I roll over

easy, shin splints searing
my bubble, like the sunflower

I reorient my suck
to chase the light

[   ]

show me
staged, what you are
wearing, the tags, the good
shit

the surplus, superimposed—all that
must riot

quiet, on my back, finally sky
omni-impotent

unholdable
I am in your hand
I am weight

.

Dear End,

In this dream I couldn't hear anything you were saying,
but I knew you were saying something. I woke up laughing.

I am jealous how you can just subtract yourself like that.
I try to expand time as not to feel it. I want total comorbidity with you.

Now, I edge myself because I don't trust you.
You want to know how your absence is affecting me?

In the dream I couldn't keep my clothes off.
Every time I rolled over they were back on.

You treat me like a crushed-out trick,
some Utopian simp.

Let's be practical,
let's move money together.

We will master laziness,
we will reproduce ourselves exquisitely.

Take loss after loss,
and lose nothing.

Decked out now, you're raining
down my asphalt.

Infected, possessed, this is how I play our game.
So come on up.

You must want entirely
or not at all,

PUMPJACK

[ ]

all my lies, they stick to
        layers of dead sea creatures
leather, thunder, voluptuous
        solidifying on the seabed
wrapped in proximity to another's skin
        buried under sedimentary rock
a brief stranger, asking for an origin
        under all that weight of stone
story and spilling cash dreams
        not even oxygen can penetrate
like ardent release, unallowable otherwise
        that deep, like a coaxed
provoking calmness, I take off his
        metaphor, trapped and becoming
belt, the paranoid distraction of
        mud and plankton and silt
extraction or guilt or pain
        and sand, salted weight
of spewing messages
        water pressed, thinner and
written in lipstick I stimulate
        partially decomposed layers
most compacted memory
        under heat of something hotter than
my lips dragging this way over
        the sun's downward pressure
finding tectonic cracks to slide through
        hips landing on air or so near death
beds of shale and earth's
        radiant ardor condensing tones
to be seen and even more

viscous, protected and engulfed
a plush fantasy marked
by impermeable rock and contained
by the storm lessons of geologic time

*

I've got thighs
fracturing, they exhale
like methane drains
in the castle infrastructure
a process all vice and bricked
time porous with injected water
to the desire bundled up
in earthquake's carbonation
sand and forbidden threshold
against the sentence wells
peering in the window from a geo time portal
the resulting fractures
in my mind, Central Valley oil fields
surround shale rock glisten thick
formations allow all ancient public footpaths
for hydrocarbons to escape
the gentle oikos and armchairs
a mixture of water, Roman fascism
American pop culture, needing
sand and chemicals to understand
itself and poetry pumped into the feed
at high pressures as clouds burn off
like untranslatable stories
that move through the imperceptible holes
tune my attention and worker catastrophe
in the casing toward global big box stores
the fluids crack open state abandoned

options narrowed down to
the shale rock and we clean our shit
together the sand holds target
the welcome portal keeps forgetting
us and there are chemicals
I forget how to pronounce
tuning the air and pumping out
a totality I can't parse out precedes
thousands of cubic feet
we feel it that's how we know it
each day

★

the rocks down there made me
millions, Adam said, oil filling
all my geologic sluts handling
these tiny dusty allowances
and interconnected spaces faking universe
Adam said, in the buried rock,
the consumption strike can't be
coordinated to produce oil,
only on the backend of
an exploration company can we destroy
what we've made. not thinking reservoir, a volume
of rock and we become with sufficient
pores, each other's oil. Adam said
be reservoir, contain water, be salary
be irresponsible, be bossed around. limit
amounts of oil or only hold water
in this rock volume the wall is there to contain
must also be surrounded so you can
let it all out like rocks that lack a stranger's
saliva in my pores which trap and alter

my DNA, a string of hollow pipes
            and all my blood that releases all at once
runs from the horse head to the reservoir
            at the bottom of the well
my spit and piss mixed with
            the hidden parts of dust, the earth of color
the sucker rod system rippled backwards
            are two simple chambers like a halo
multiplied that seal with ball valves
            or unbearable sound, the valve on a plunger
if I were that unbearable sound, raw and opens as
            the rod system moves made of stars
downward allowing oil to fill money and
            the plunger and forces & destroys my names
the fluids in the pipe and all echoing vows
            above it upward and upward

★

it could be that I am a well or was one once
            I feel my soft skin against a factory thong
dirt evicted in a dugout core on stolen land
            the plywood weaved around
Chevron's unliberated future scenarios and
            the rupture's most adorned ATM stance
corporate specs that hold hostage
            anyone who sees us can't see us
wrecked workers and climate's deathyawn
            sparking reclaimed withdrawal fees
glugging their own obsolescence
            metal to blood vessel to worn out elastic
with occupied flow stations against US presence
            armed assassins dream in neon
state sanctioned private security protects white

76

life and declined credit cards carved
to extinguish right then and there
    with hunted risk & glands substantial
any as if, any no never, any dispersal refusal
    that demands the uncutting of mineral
rights from grazing rights to water rites
    agreed on in throngs, unassimilated
whose incision demarcates a national grid
    our summed and fractioned tactics
on some superfund site that banks on
    colluding clouds and later the flash flood
erosion's ill-will to hold up the legal platform
    no matter what the broken clocks are
spewing refinery's wasted spill
    right twice a day invisible
from the global delta heaving death
    the state's zippers caked in lucite cum
stopping struggle by worker manual to download
    velvet corpses, polluted, unassimilable each unit
our aromas muzzled together
    a Luddite tactic too heavy to lift
lulling tariffed cargo with uninsured joints
    murderous orators in ecstasy
of pipeline gas to the destruction of the throat
    of respective war furniture
mocking my intimate infrastructure
    converging we annihilate each other
as workers & state IDs we annihilate
    the verification system we annihilate
the shackled fantasy of aching feet, adrenal shame
    and lip liner in the cozy hour molding fantasy of intimacy
how oil money rots virile our pleasure leaking to the front-end strike
    and back-end theft slipping through power
intertwined throes death sleep in charred windows

tethered inseparable the future's organismic
demand, immanent in each other's eyes together
all guts and rosy, tucked and seeping

[   ]

O today's the day
after yesterday
and the unlikely water
boils the ungrateful shore

childlike clouds brag rain
on carpet floor, our garden
of keys, fracking desire into
renewable haze

fudging monsoon, rewriting
drainage maps and disputed property
signs, I ride with luck and
stamina, behind
enemy lines

here Adam no longer believes
in the state's death
and I orbit carefully
how power forges
his daydream, represses
his doomsday

leaders invent new workdays
to echo mirror language
into Adam's gag reflex,
and I've trained mine
to stay calm while tears
swim upstream

an oiled down Edenic bitch
for drippy shale gas
companies jerking unconscious
to offload apples and apples
from necro orchards of
Trees of Knowledge

devil shit to dig
that deeply into the earth,
to rub one out
to chevron my engine
in daddy's ghost
town, our century's
missing origin

tonight I work
to hate Adam's order
in order to fill our
little room, yes I eat
Adam's order in order
to strip his state
pockets perfectly

[   ]

the rock is permeable. most rock
except when it's pushed to the limit.
erosion trips the sun dial to an amount
only the Law can measure, as if the future
could be accounted for with numbers that stay
on their side of the bed.

even though I was older, I always thought
you were. I looked to you for answers like
what if there is beauty, and you aren't there
to receive it? define heaping. just before it begins
to hurt. if I evaluate you within a degree of perfection,
will that prove my love?

so I began to claw
at paving stones. stardust slams
our present. Velocity. take the city apart.
Velocity. you are good at controlling
the pace at which the horizon arrives.

you are willing to walk away,
which makes you closer to me
than I am. when you clock my compulsion
it's in the palm of your hand. like a busted
lock, the phone is ringing. Velocity.

despair makes a hero out of me, so I get
busy, fly around an untangled sun, up
End my-self, donate my organs to the poets.

earth creaks blatantly, asking

for help. hands crumbling, sprinting
surfaces. Velocity. once you lap me,
I can finally let you. it used to be
much simpler.

This is how everyday words become love songs.
I straddle our distance and ride.

I sing a ballad of spores. I climb your heart's rank.
Stars make me trust light, never having truly arrived.

It is possible to touch without touching—
you know better than anyone,

how to distinguish a relic from what's at work.
I'm ready to air out my false consciousness, all I covet.

I'm a habituated creature. I always thank my objects,
not as a political horizon, but as an honest feeling.

I set myself in motion.
It's not that I chase you, it's that you cause me to chase.

Crass retention, I wave your flags, my true pleasure.
I build barricades in front of my desire, I halt my ruddy poethics.

I cough with hunger for you.
Attaching my dorsal fin to your not knowing.

Refracting daddy, I'll spend all I've got,
pour my debt into your debt's glass,

Steady loudness, rhythmic collapse. Maniacal
with programmatic visions. Your immanence reigns.

But like you said, the sonnetman
only comes to regulate our futures,

LIMIT

[   ]

and suddenly our love became
common. I climbed I-5 going
90 as if that would prove it.
how wholly I could be without
you. in dreams our childhood
houses merged, I was neither guest
nor home. that day I shattered
my glass, my fist was made
of years. watching us, it showed
up on skin, spelling it out. my
skin. I swear to god how could you
with your chest. so salt eroded
your face, betrayed our will, our
will, flat on our backs. my back.
Gravitron kids sick with how could I
prove it. how wholly I couldn't be
without you. complicit horizon,
stupid speed, stupid symptom.

every night the mosquito
eats my jaw. time cracks, it
flowers. and no state of frozen
could expand each bone out
of my sorry vessel, all
omniscience, no evidence.

and isn't it common. what we did,
we did so well, so well,
there was no way, no
way, no way there was no
way

[   ]

I never said I'm not truth to you.
the wind can't lift the wings of
the frozen goldfinch, tucked in next
to the shitty ice cubes, old ice cream.
when it was time to move, I dug
a grave with a silver spoon that bent
against soil, wringed neck, six
months after I never said it could be
that two things can be true,
one year after we slammed into
the window. as if animals could
make mistakes. I never thought it would
go on this long, for forever. I never
thought the plane could draw that note,
the metal could never consent
to break, a body could ever
break, I could never type
resurrection in the thesaurus
looking for the weakest match.
never said I couldn't make you
laugh harder. never said I wasn't
dying, never said I haven't refreshed
your name how many times. never said
I wouldn't pay for it.

I was burying you when you called.
swallowing your note, I wasn't
whispering comeback kid come
back. hot water thick dirt yellow wing
come back kid I never said come

[   ]

alterations, crickets, fixer uppers

I ripped off the symphony
to master the back float,
sold off the bird corpses and couch
cushions, the rot I covet, the indices
of exhaustion. I did not know
how clean you could shave, just how close,
how you trusted your blood to clot. ice
swarmed my throat, filled with god, I choked
it down. like poison, toward middle earth.
I practiced my sermons in thick and juicy
time.

it's possible I am a mealworm,
watching images of sky ripped open,
not comprehending the quantum shock
that wears down all of our bodies.

grace breaks like dawn. I couldn't tell
why I was crying at the funeral. you
were trying to cover your tracks,
and I let you.

I made you Zeus
so I could pout tauter than a ratchet strap,
like a vine lung bound. time clefts and screeches,
there is no death that could suture us, no oath
era to root our mothers and like a child I am sorry
for static sleep, to swallow and be swallowed.
it's a devastating grammar—what cannot repeat.

cracked by questions, by believing we could know
less by white knuckling excessive certainty
from the inside out—

chasm demanded us, so we chasmed—

and if we see each other on the other side,
I promised myself to ask no questions
about what happened to you along the way,
I will only know that you are here

[ ]

infinity returned. I experienced time
for the first time as the thickness of our plot rolled
out over the Carrizo Plain's skeletal seaside. that red
carpet dust road made me feel so summa sine laude
with you. no separate selves / no cattle in sight. out there
dust's shadow made us indistinguishable like I like it.
a lullaby catches on fire in the desertified August.
it's moony salt bush begging engine heat's flames. remember?
when the truck refused tinder bundle bouquets and we got suspended
good, an offroad stampede. steaming piss and a new view
of what we were seeking, in the fault lines of our fatty depth.

everything there the untouchable color of your hair, when I scroll that
euphoria it's this golden block of missing cows and your grown
out roots. the steak cut lesson branded my disturbed loyalty,
precluded my world view of earth. driving into nothing, swallowed
mist dries up, blazing balls and metal trophs, stolen water seeps
into oranges growing complicit with the vitamins we forage.
krinked plateau thrills like there is no end the thickness of our
Kármán line. we live in each other's anajuridical edge. we've pooled
our viral loads, tagged the pre-Homeric marginalia in our marrow.

out here in this lonely space walk you taught me metalaw:
treat others how they desire to be. you treat my desire as many godly.
your love blisters my army to break any weaponed walls and sense.
sparkling cache of rowdy delicatessens. leg locked self-help boored into
me as I am never not entering the stream of your dubbed out
gaze. I've clipped my cosmic tether to you, you write the fuel
of my jetpack, conduct my RPMs of Jello shots, sing me Tara Brach.
liberatory pranks with more solar wind than physics can tame.
you air drop me to me, beyond the speed of Bakersfield sound.

imagine thinking stars are just those little dots. your light slams me
at the velocity of your overhand, shattering my secretarial
systems, it rolls out BIG like spilling breakers, quiet and rideable
and always in my cluttered sense of loveability. loving you
in the mode your being spills into the heightened state
of a mouth's meditating rave. excess dribbling on plumped
out lips, mouthing the fake flu and universal clues, your forehead
can't freeze my catalogue of ships. I idle till the cop's printer runs out
of paper to ticket me, singing contraband contradiction, tennis court adieu
or almond goo. with you I know time goes back longer than unassimilated
years of being mother-molded, toward being made to weave our own gravity.

ACKNOWLEDGEMENTS / AFTERMATH

The end is a theoretical crisis, a temporal impossibility. The truth is it always keeps going. It has been here the whole time. The etymology of apocalypse is *revelation*: to remove the veil, to reveal. What's underneath has always been carved in the sky. Every letter is purloined, the death drive is actually on the side of life. Just like everyone here is, to whom I consider it a great fortune to be indebted.

Thank you to Nightboat Books staff for taking such good care of this book. Stephen Motika, for entering this manuscript so deeply with me. Lindsey Boldt, Gia Gonzales, Lina Bergamini, Emily Bark Brown, Dante Silva, Trisha Low, Naima Yael Tokunow, Santiago Valencia, Kit Schluter, Morgan Levine, Jaye Elizabeth Elijah. Thank you Rissa Hochberger, for etching my shield as always.

Poetry Club You Save(d) My Life: Tess Brown-Lavoie, Kayla Ephros, Emily Martin, Mary Clark, Ivanna Baranova. Thank you for spending so much time with these poems. You hold me, you write me, you feel me.

I wrote many of these poems in Poetry Project workshops and rogue poetry schools over the past few years. Gratitude to the offerings from Ben Krusling's "world, interrupted," Kay Gabriel's Bernadette Mayer workshop "Eat Everything," Tiana Reid's "Crush Redux," Elaine Kahn's Poetry Field School, and Ted Rees' Overflowing Workshop. Thank you to Apogee Graphics where I finished this manuscript.

Thank you in particular to Irene Silt, Nora Treatbaby, Ted Rees, Grace Nissan, and Cyrus Dunham. Your notes helped me sculpt this book and therefore understand myself.

Versions of these poems have appeared in *Baest: a journal of queer forms and affects*, *Blazing Stadium*, *Tripwire*, *Berkeley Poetry Review*, *Spoil IV*, and *ATM Magazine*. Many of these poems appear in *Pumpjack*, (2021). Gratitude comrades for keeping poetry alive.

To my friends, shifting galaxies of care. For your collusion, for your love, for letting me crash. The first five poems in "Contact Potential" were written in correspondence with Sacha Maccabee, my blameless tennis partner & collaborator in the lifelong lesson: to have Love is to have lost. *L'œuf all*. The rest is floated by the conversation and care of many, but especially: James, my primary care provider. Noa, cloud, miracle. Nora, this shit's unthinkable w out you. Evie, your immanence. Infinite Elizabeth, you are home, you are Bakersfield. And Cy, may this love continue to find new, unbreakable forms.

Mom, Dad, Liz, Katy, Ben. With every year I come to understand with stark clarity how your love shapes and supports me.

Thank you highways, thank you gas, thank you sky, thank you body, thank you earth—for refusal, for life.

Finally, to every pipeline protest, decolonial struggle, and resistance for a free Palestine.

NOTES

This book reverbs with the words of others, my most extimate relations. Of all the traceable loose ends in this book I especially recommend: Ovid, *Metamorphosis*. Bernadette Mayer, "Soule Sermon." Arthur Rimbaud, *Illuminations*. Karl Marx, *Capital Vol. 1*. Saidiya Hartman, *Wayward Lives, Beautiful Experiments*. Diane di Prima, *Revolutionary Letters*. Jacques Lacan, *Desire and its Interpretation*. Denise Ferreira da Silva, *Unpayable Debt*. William Blake, *The Complete Poems*.

"Loose Ends" is a translation-by-memory of "Phrases" by Arthur Rimbaud, *Illuminations*, trans. Wallace Fowlie.

The phrase "Carmen Et Error" is a reference to the reason Ovid was exiled from Rome, which he claimed was *carmen et error*: "a poem and a mistake" in *Ovid: The Poems Of Exile (Tristia, Ex Ponto, Ibis)*, trans. A. S. Kline.

The phrase "we became what we beheld" in ["this poem to be plundered"] is a reference to William Blake's "Jerusalem: The Emanation of the Giant Albion."

["like a line that doesn't Regulate"] is a cento made up of words from the Wikipedia entry on the Kármán line.

In ["O host itch"] the phrase "man of twists and returns" is a play off the first description of Odysseus in Homer's *The Odyssey*, trans. Robert Fagles: "a man of twists and turns."

The form of the first poems in "Pumpjack" is taken from Bernadette Mayer's poem "Soule Sermon" in *Works and Days*, which interweaves the lines of two different poems. The first set of lines in "Pumpjack" are taken from *The Story of Oil* by Walter Sheldon Tower about the history of the petroleum industry.

ROSIE STOCKTON is the author of *Permanent Volta* (2021) and *Pumpjack* (2022). They hold an M.A. in Creative Writing from Eastern Michigan University and are a Ph.D. Candidate in the Gender Studies Department at UCLA. Rosie lives and works in Los Angeles.

NIGHTBOAT BOOKS

Nightboat Books, a nonprofit organization, seeks to develop audiences for writers whose work resists convention and transcends boundaries. We publish books rich with poignancy, intelligence, and risk. Please visit nightboat.org to learn about our titles and how you can support our future publications.

The following individuals have supported the publication of this book. We thank them for their generosity and commitment to the mission of Nightboat Books:

Kazim Ali
Anonymous (4)
Ava Aviva Avnisan
Jean C. Ballantyne
Will Blythe
V. Shannon Clyne
Theodore Cornwell
Ulla Dydo Charitable Fund
Gisela Gamper
Photios Giovanis
Amanda Greenberger
David Groff
Parag Rajendra Khandhar
Katy Lederer

Shari Leinwand
Elizabeth Madans
Ricardo Maldonado
Ethan Mitchell
Caren Motika
Elizabeth Motika
Asker Saeed
The Leslie Scalapino - O Books Fund
Amy Scholder
Thomas Shardlow
Benjamin Taylor
Jerrie Whitfield & Richard Motika
Clay Williams

This book is made possible, in part, by grants from the National Endowment for the Arts, New York City Department of Cultural Affairs in partnership with the City Council, the New York State Council on the Arts Literature Program, and the Topanga Fund, which is dedicated to promoting the arts and literature of California.